About this Book

Virtually everyone now has access to a HD video camera. Most smartphones and even the cheapest compact cameras are capable of shooting quality video that would've been unbelievable 10 years ago. Now ultra-high definition (4K) is starting to become more accessible too, and the ability to easily take and share video is creating whole new ways of making and viewing video content.

In this book, we're going to look at what you can do to improve the kind of videos you make specifically to upload and share on the internet; how to make them better technically, and generally more professional.

Many of the simple editing and production skills we cover apply to any kind of video work, but we'll focus particularly on elements that will help you create effective demonstration videos, vlogs and interviews. We'll also look at how to capture video gaming footage to produce live commentary gaming videos. We'll show you the basics that you need to know to make your videos stand out - for the right reasons!

It's recommended that when following this book you have the appropriate app on screen.

About the Authors

John Chatwin is a sociologist who works in the field of communication and visual methods. He runs a video production company - Visible Research - which specialises in research and dissemination films, primarily for internet delivery.

Oscar Chatwin is a keen YouTuber with a particular interest in Gaming and Gaming videos. He has wide experience of making and uploading videos to his channel Ronocon.

Trademarks

Contents

1 Video production software

Choosing software that's right for you

Good editing and production software is essential if you are going to make the most of your videos. There are scores of different applications available ranging from programmes and apps that are basically free to use, right through to fully professional packages that can handle the complete production process.

How you choose which software to use really depends on what your production needs are likely to be. If you're only interested in editing the odd bit of holiday video to stick on YouTube then something very basic will be fine.

If you're more serious about things, you'll want to think about using a more professionally featured package. Most of the ones in the following list are available as free trial downloads, although there are likely to be some limitations, either on how long you can use the application before you have to buy it, or on some of the functions you can access. Any of these will easily handle the simple production processes we'll be describing though, even in trial mode.

The programmes we've chosen are only a few of those available, but they represent ones that would probably crop up in an average top ten of popular applications.

Adobe Premiere Pro CC

Adobe Premiere Pro Creative Cloud (CC) is one of the most widely used professional production packages for PCs and it's now also available for Macs.

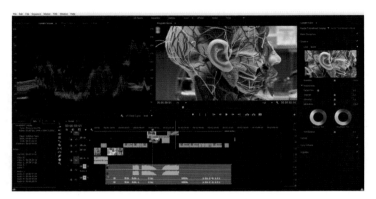

It has a wide range of powerful features, and a clean, clear interface. Although on its own it can handle virtually any video production challenge you can throw at it, it also integrates directly with a suite of other Adobe programmes including After Effects, which is a visual effects and motion graphics application that's used for compositing and animation. Photoshop and Dreamweaver are also part this collection.

Download the trial version at:
https://creative.adobe.com/products/download/premiere

Main user forums:
https://forums.adobe.com/community/premiere

Apple Final Cut Pro X

If you're using a Mac, Final Cut has been an industry standard for many years. Like Adobe Premier, it's certainly not cheap, and it's not exactly a programme for beginners. However, it is fairly intuitive to use if you've had a little experience of generic video editing enviroments, and has far more capabilities than you'll ever need.

Another plus feature is the huge formal and informal support community you can access that isn't just limited to professionals.

Although these can be cliquey and fairly annoying to engage with, if you're prepared to poke about a bit you can usually find what you need to know.

Download the trial version at:
http://www.apple.com/final-cut-pro/trial/

Main support forum:
https://discussions.apple.com/community/professional_applications/final_cut_pro_x

DaVinci Resolve

DaVinci Resolve is a slick professional production package that's available in free and purchased versions for PC and Mac.

In the free version all of the essential – and many advanced – features can be used without any restrictions, although some of the 3D editing functions are disabled, along with motion blur and image noise reduction. This makes Resolve a very popular choice, particularly as it'll handle all of the common formats as well as almost all types of RAW (i.e. high quality, un-compressed) camera files.

Download:
http://www.blackmagicdesign.com/uk/products/davinciresolve

VEGAS Movie Studio 14

This was developed out of the original Sony Vegas editing software and is simple to use, basic and clear. It doesn't really have the professional 'feel' of Premier or Final Cut, but it's got plenty of usable features. It's reasonably priced and ideal for a beginner.

There are also higher specification versions: **Movie Studio Platinum** and **Movie Studio Suite**, which offer more features such as colour correction and advanced titling options.

Download:

http://www.vegascreativesoftware.com/us/vegas-movie-studio/

Corel Videostudio Pro X10 and Videostudio Ultimate X10

As with Vagas Movie Studio, although they have some advanced capabilities, these two packages are really aimed at the consumer market. They are basic and easy to use, without any of the esoteric features or control you'd expect to find in more professional applications.

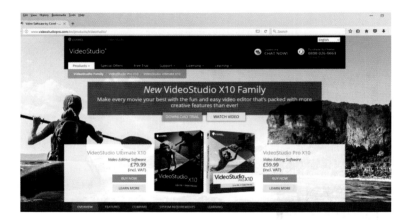

They do have some useful effects and processes such as automatic noise reduction, and there is even stop motion, freeze frame and multi-point motion tracking.

These programmes are fine if you're on a tight budget or you just do occasional simple editing. The user interface and workflow process are similar to higher spec programmes, so you shouldn't find upgrading to something more serious much of a problem.

Download:
http://www.corel.com/en/free-trials/

Hit Film 4 Express

The software we'll be using for the examples in this book is Hit Film 4 Express. If you are new to video production the software is relatively easy get to grips with, but still has a very professional feel. And unlike most of the other full feature software you'll come across, even the 'free' edition maintains the majority of functions that you'll need to use – certainly at this level.

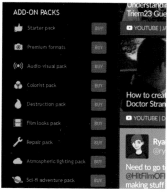

If you want to go deeper into things there are reasonably priced add-ons that can be downloaded to add extra capabilities. The starter pack (£8.00 at time of writing) for example, provides advanced colour correction and grading functions, along with various audio and video effects processors.

Downloading and installing

Hit Film 4 Express is available to download from the developer's at:

https://hitfilm.com/express

Follow the link above. It will take you to the home page. Scroll down through the glossy pictures of the developers posing about with expensive film gear and click on the blue bar that says get film express free. The content of these pages tends to be updated regularly, so they won't necessarily look exactly as shown here.

The main download page

This will take you through the rest of the download process. You will be asked to create an account by giving your email and making up a password. There are also some questions about what you plan to use the programme for. Click on send me the download and the system will send an email to the address you specified (so no point just making one up).

This email contains a final link that sends you to a page where you can specify what kind of download you need (i.e. Windows or Mac). Then you'll be able to actually start the download process.

Choosing the correct download format

Once you've got the programme, it should appear in your downloads folder. At time of writing, the filename is: HitFilm4Express_4.0.5609.1082. Although revisions and updates are fairly constant, so the version number is likely to change. If the installer doesn't start automatically, find the file and click on it to start it manually.

Find the installer in your downloads folder

The download registration screen

Run the programme by double clicking on it and follow the on screen instructions to complete the installation. You will then need to activate the software. Do this by actually opening Hit Film 4 Express. The installer should have put an icon on your desktop, but it will also show up in your start menu if you are using Windows 7 - 10.

Windows 10 start menu

Fill in the email and password that you provided at the beginning. Click Activate and you should be good to go. You will only be able to install a single copy of the programme registered to a particular email address, so if you need to swap computers for any reason you will be asked to de-activate any existing installations when you activate. In practice though, as long as you are connected to the internet (and you would need to be anyway to download the installation software) this is very straightforward.

Minimum system requirements

Like virtually all video production software, HF4 is a power hungry programme, which in some ways is reassuring. However it does mean that if your computer is even mildly under spec you are going to run into trouble. This wil be especially evident if you try and edit 4K video files. The programme should be able to handle them, but even on a good spec average machine it's likely to be infuriatingly slow and basically unusable. On the Hit Film website they outline the minimum and recommended specifications needed to run sessions effectively. These are:

- Windows 7, Windows 8, Windows 10, OS X 10.9 Mavericks, OS X 10.10 Yosemite or OS X 10.11 El Capitan
- 64-bit operating system
- 1 GB free hard disk space for installation
- Internet connection required for online activation
- Intel Core i3, Core i5, Core i7 or Intel Xeon (Nehalem) processor or AMD equivalent
- 4GB RAM
- OpenGL 2.0 capable hardware with at least 512 MB vid memory (NVIDIA GeForce 9 series, Radeon HD 5000 series, Intel HD 4000)

On the face of it, these requirements are not particularly demanding and many reasonably up to date consumer PCs should be able to match them. However, in researching this book we tried installing it on several different machines, ranging from mid-range i5 laptops through to the top spec i7 PC we usually use for video production. Results were mixed. Basically, if you try and run HF4 on anything with less than an i5 3rd generation CPU and 8 GB of RAM you are likely to be faced with ultra-slow performance and frequent crashes. That's if it starts at all.

GTX 1080 Graphics Card
High end graphics can improve video performance, but unless the rest of your PC is equally high spec, you may not see much improvement.

A decent video card is also essential if you are going to achieve anything like a practical working speed, and the on-board graphics found in many consumer PCs (which usually need to hog a portion of system RAM) may not be up to the job.

As most people reading this book are unlikely to want to spend a lot of time and money building a dedicated video editing PC it's probably best to just download the software and see if your computer can handle it. As with all things computer related, issues of compatibility and performance can seem infuriatingly random, and it may just work without any problems.

2 Shooting guidelines

In this book we're mainly concerned with helping you to improve the kind of video content that you'll be uploading to sites like YouTube or sharing on social media; maybe you need to make a short promo for embedding in a website, or you want to make your vlog more professional looking. Although the things that you need to consider when making this kind of content are usually fairly straightforward there are a few basic 'rules' and conventions common to most types of video and film-making that you'll need to know (even if you choose not to follow them). These will help make your videos easier to edit and produce, and ultimately better to watch.

Planning and preparation

This may seem obvious but having a definite idea about what it is you want to produce and how you want it to look well in advance is essential. Even if you just plan to film yourself sitting at a desk for a video diary or vlog, there are things to sort out first if you don't want to look amateurish: what equipment are you going to use and how are you going to set it up?; are you planning to just film it on your smartphone or have you got a camcorder or DSLR you could use; will you need to use extra lighting?; how will you set that up?; what about the sound? Recording decent sound is essential for professional results (see chapter 6), so you'll need to work out how you're going to record it. What are you going to say? A lot of vlogs are deliberately informal and seemingly off the cuff, but you should at least do a bit of a rehearsal to warm up and check things like shot composition and sound are how you want them.

Along with the practical things such as sound and lighting, for more complicated productions like promotional videos, or demonstration videos that may have certain essential shots, proper planning is vital. If you don't want to waste a lot of time and end up with hours of unusable footage, you need to have a good idea how you want the finished video to look – which shots you have to get and how you plan to use them – before you start.

This becomes more important if you'll only have limited time in a particular location. For even the simplest production it pays to work out a basic shooting script beforehand (basically just an ordered list of shots) so that you can check you've got all the footage you need. Then there may be practical details such as the nature of a location that you need to think about. Perhaps you'll need permission in advance to film there? If you plan to interview people – even for informal vox pops – you should know exactly what it is you need to ask them. Be prepared to explain what you are doing and how their comments will be used.

Avoid fast zooms and panning

When you look at a lot of material on the internet – particularly music videos – the old established rules of camera work are constantly sub-verted. Excessive zooming is a good example. When it's done intention-ally, as part of an overall style, it can be fine. Some styles of documen-tary and reality video deliberately use it to add a sense of immediacy and pace. The same goes for fast panning, but again, unless it's used as part of a consistent overall editing style it'll probably just look rubbish.

Get lots of cut-aways

Cutaways simply let you cut away from the action or interview subject and maintain a sense of continuity by avoiding disconcerting jump cuts. Cutaways can be virtually anything – shots of a person's hands, a shot of them from across the room doing whatever they're doing.

In an interview, you might want to edit together two short comments from someone, but if you simply stick them one after the other it can look as if the person suddenly moves (a jump-cut). Deliberate jump-cuts are quite trendy now - particulalry in vlogs, but if you are making a more conventional narrative based video and want to keep things looking smooth and professional you can use a cutaway to hide the cut and create a sequence that looks more like one continuous comment.

Two camera side cut-away

Another trendy way of shooting interviews at the moment is to set up a normal face-on shot with the interviewee looking slightly off to one side, and have another camera shooting them in profile. The face on view will be your main shot, and the side view lets you do cut-aways that are synchronised with it.

These cut-aways are essentially just stylistic, so if you don't have two decent cameras to spare you can sometimes make do with a lower spec camera for the side shot – even a smartphone – and make a feature of the contrasting picture quality in the cut-away. Some people go further and put the cut-away in black and white or generally mess about with it in other ways.

Swap sides

If you are going to video formal interviews with more than one person in the same location, it's good to change the position of the camera for each person to avoid possible jump-cuts later on. If you video one person facing right, do the next one facing left. This will give you more options when you edit.

Cutting straight from shot A to shot B could create the impression of an unintentional jump-cut. Both shots are framed the same and look fairly similar. You will draw attention to what might otherwise be a smooth (i.e. unnoticed) transition.

Cutting between shots C and D creates less of a distracting jump. The interviewees are facing in different directions, and even though the background is the same, the effect will be much smoother

Don't cross the line

'Crossing the line' is something else you want to avoid. Basically, if you're filming from one direction, you don't want your next shot to be looking back at where your camera would've been. This can be distracting and easily create problems with spatial relationships.

For example, if you are filming two people having a conversation and you want to be able to cut from one to the other for reaction shots, you should imagine a line going through them both, following their line of vision. Then make sure your camera positions are all on the same side of that line.

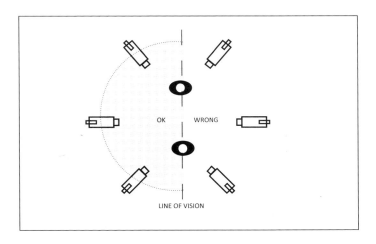

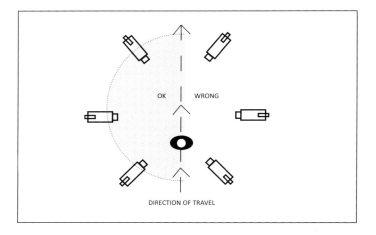

This rule also works for live action and can help you avoid reverse cuts which occur when the camera crosses the line of action, or the direction in which the subject is moving.

Interviewing

In a lot of interview situations, whether formally set up, or out in the street, it usually looks better to get an interviewee to look slightly to one side of the camera, rather than straight at it. This is particularly true if the person isn't used to being filmed. Looking straight at a camera can be very unnerving for people and really emphasises distracting eye movements. It can make them look uncomfortable and shifty, even if they aren't. Professional actors and presenters are trained to hold their gaze firmly on the camera, and avoid moving their eyes about too much.

When you're interviewing someone, it's best to get them to make eye contact with you as they are speaking, so that you can hold their gaze and help them to avoid looking at the camera. This will obviously mean you need to stand in line with where you want them to look.

If you are filming and recording sound as well, it can be tricky to monitor everything, so it's good to tell the person that occasionally you will need to check the camera, and that if this happens you have not lost interest in what they are saying, and they should carry on talking to the spot where you were standing - maybe even make a mark on the wall behind you that they can line up with.

Unless you're working with professional actors, it's best not to try and get people to remember and rehearse exactly what they want to say. Certainly, avoid letting anyone read out anything on camera because it looks terrible, and even if you think you may be able to salvage something to use as a voice over it will usually come across as wooden. Some people will naturally be very good at doing this type of thing, but unless you've got plenty of time to try different approaches it's best to play safe.

Get plenty of natural sound

This can really be a life saver. If you're filming anywhere that has ambient background noise always make sure that you record at least a couple of minutes of natural sound. This is usually called a 'wild track', and just means sound that isn't synchronised to any particular bit of film or video.

If you're making a video in a workshop, for example, get the sounds

of different types of machinery working, along with quieter recordings of general activity. If you're filming an event, you should get a few minutes of the general murmur of the audience waiting for the performance to start, some applause, laughter etc.

Even if there's no overt 'noise' in a location, just record the general

ambience. Having a good wild track that matches the atmosphere of a location can be invaluable in smoothing out audio transitions and helping to make seamless sequences.

Simple lighting set-ups

Three point lighting is used a lot in video production – particularly for interviews and other situations where you need to film people's faces. The idea is that you create an even and flattering effect where shadows define the features but don't overpower them.

As you might expect, a three-point set-up needs three lights: a **key light**; a **fill light**; and a **back light**. The key is the main light, and you'd usually place it at around 45 degrees to the subject, and slightly to the left or right of the camera. On its own, the key will create some defining shadows, but if there are no other lights, these are likely to be too dark and un-flattering. This is why a fill light is also used.

The fill is usually dimmer than the key, and will often be a soft light, or have some degree of diffusion. Its role is to balance out the deeper shadows created by the key light and give a more even effect. Start by placing it roughly 45 degrees to the subject, but on the opposite side of the camera to the key, and move it around to get the effect you want.

A back light can be as bright as, or brighter than the key, and is placed facing down onto the back of the subject's head and shoulders. The back light helps to isolate the subject from their background and create a more three-dimensional effect.

If you only have one light – and a lot of video work is done with only one – position it as you would a key light.

You can often make use of natural light coming from windows or room lights, but remember to set the white balance on your camera to match whatever combination you may end up with.

Magic Lantern

The trend towards using DSLRs for video work may not be as strong as it was now that dedicated camcorders offering many of the features that attracted people to use DSLRs for video are more widely available. These included 'filmlike' video quality – particularly the narrow depth of field that video cameras often struggle with – the ability to use professional lenses, and with some cameras, access to the whole range of manual functions from the stills camera.

There are still many video and film makers using DSLRs because of the versatility and picture quality they offer, and a whole sub-culture of users has developed around this. One particular aspect of this has seen enthusiasts trying to reverse engineer the firmware controlling their cameras so that they can open up even more functionality and control.

Magic Lantern is a free software add-on that runs on most Canon EOS cameras. Similar projects have been attempted with the other main professional brands, but difficulties in unpicking the firmware used by manufacturers such as Nikon has meant that there isn't any serious Magic Lantern equivalent. Certainly, none that have been refined to such a high degree.

> **WARNING**
>
> It is possible - although according to most of the ML forums, unlikely - that by tampering with the firmware controlling your camera you could cause permanent damage. You will almost certainly invalidate your warranty, so think before you unzip any files. . .

If you have a Canon and don't mind running the possible risk of damaging your camera and invalidating your warranty, ML can open up some fantastic video and audio functions. These include include manual audio, zebras (useful for showing peak levels of exposure within a shot), focus assist tools, bracketing and motion detection.

You can download Magic Lantern at:
http://www.magiclantern.fm/

Magic Lantern homepage

Magic Lantern is modified firmware that runs in the background on the camera's memory card. It doesn't actually make any changes to the original camera firmware. When you turn the camera on, rather than loading its factory default, it detects that there is firmware on the memory card and boots up using that.

If you want to run the camera as normal you simply swap to a memory card that isn't loaded with Magic Lantern and re-boot. Magic Lantern is only a small file (usually around 2MB) so even when uncompressed it takes up very little card space. If you want to get rid of it completely you simply format the card and the camera will revert back to booting up with its factory installed firmware.

Downloading Magic Lantern

If you scroll down to the bottom of the Magic Lantern home page, you'll find the download link. This will take you to the 'nightly builds' page where you'll see a list of the different EOS camera versions that are supported. These range from Canon's pro flagship 5D Mark 111, through to much older models such as the 500D / Rebel T1i.

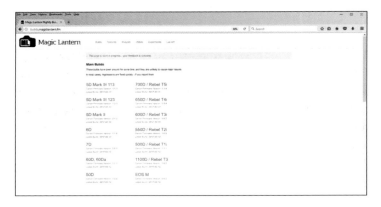

The process is much the same for all models, but there are variations in the particular functions that might be available. The version for the 650D that we're using here, for example, does not have some of the audio features (such as dynamic level metering) found in most other versions.

MAGIC LANTERN

These variations are because all of the development work on Magic Lantern is essentially done by enthusiasts, and a quirk of design thrown into the mix – in this case an audio chip that seems to be used only in the 650D – can mean that previously matched coding that worked with other models isn't compatible. The time and effort needed to reverse engineer the firmware for this specific quirk in an older camera has meant that it's become a low priority for people. It's difficult to moan about this because, as the developers point out, no one is getting paid to work on ML, so if you want to improve certain things, download the firmware and hack into it yourself!

Installation

Before you can do anything, you need to see that your're running the correct Canon firmware version. This is specified on the download page and can be checked by looking in the settings menu on your camera. Magic lantern won't run unless you have the right firmware version. If you try to load it alongside incompatible versions, the red LED will flash and you may need to take the battery out to reset things, but it shouldn't damage your camera.

To begin the install, you will need access to a PC to download the ML zip file, and a card reader to copy them to your memory card. You will also need to have a fully charged battery in the camera.

1) Set the mode dial to the Manual (M) position, and re-set the camera to its default settings. Then double check that you have the correct Canon firmware version (in this case version 1.0.4, displayed at the bottom of the fourth tools menu).

2) Tick the 'low-level' dialogue box on the format screen, and perform a low-level format to clear your memory card (this must be done in the camera). Then put it in your PC card reader, or an externally connected one.

3) Download the relevant zip file of Magic Lantern that you need from the downloads page.

4) Put the card back in the camera and do a firmware update. The options for doing this will be in your tools menu – probably in a sub-screen related to the firmware version. Then re-start your camera.

Once you've done this you should be able to toggle between the enhanced Magic Lantern functions by pressing the delete or bin button, although this may vary depending on the model.

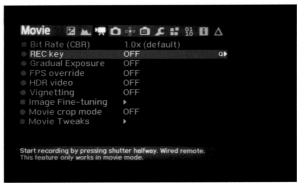

Installing Magic Lantern can be a bit daunting, but all the help and information you need, along with a very vibrant user community is on the developer's website. It's not recommended for beginners!

http://wiki.magiclantern.fm/install

3 Basic video editing

In this section we're going to show you how to import video files and work with them in your video editor. We'll be using some basic editing functions so that you can see how clips can be put together to make simple sequences, and how a standard timeline based interface works.

We're going to be using Hit Film 4 as our editing software. If you're using a different application, such as Adobe Premier or Davinci Resolve, you'll find functions such as importing and cutting clips, moving them around in relation to one another, and applying transitions, are all achieved in a fairly standard way.

More advanced functions such as splitting audio and video tracks, controlling how effects are applied, or working with key frames (see page 60) may be trickier to figure out, but there are plenty of online guides to help you. These programmes can be overwhelming at first, so it's mainly a question of knowing exactly what you want to achieve before you start and focusing on finding out how to use a particular function.

Some editing conventions

Before we look at the practical process of using video editing soft-ware, here are a few simple conventions to keep in mind when start-ing to edit. As with any creative process, these 'rules' are constantly being broken and subverted, and different techniques come in and out of fashion. But what we've listed here are some of the classic elements that will help you make smoother, more watchable se-quences. Of course, this may be exactly what you want to avoid!

Always cut mid-action.

In traditional editing a key aim is to make cuts and transitions between clips as inconspicuous as possible. Motion can be a way of diverting attention away from a cut. So, for example, if you have a close-up and a long shot of a person using a hammer, you should cut in the middle of the movement - when the hammer is halfway down, then start the following shot with the hammer at the same position. This makes the transition much less noticeable.

Unless you have a particular need to do so, you should also generally avoid having empty frames within a sequence, and cut away before a person leaves the frame.

Reverse Shots

If you are trying to show a natural progression of events, using a reverse shot can be useful. For example, you might have a shot of someone moving towards a shop doorway. You could then cut to a shot from inside the shop of the person at the door. This helps to create a smooth and logical sequence.

Jump cuts

A jump cut is when you have two successive shots from the same camera position, but the subject changes. A good example might be an interview where a few seconds between comments has been edited out. The interviewee will have moved during those seconds, even if only slightly. But when the two shots are cut together they will appear to jump, making it obvious that a section of footage is missing. While in conventional editing the discontinuity of a jump-cut is generally to be avoided, they are used widely – particularly in vlogs – to create a kind of deliberately (?) chopped up effect.

Use different angles

When putting together a sequence of shots from multiple angles, always try to follow a given shot with one where the angle is different by at least 45 degrees.

Otherwise, the consecutive shots may appear too similar and can create the effect of an unintended jump cut. You can combine shots of different focal length (for example a medium shot followed by a close-up) to achieve the same variation.

Fades and dissolves

Basic editing cuts are known as 'hard cuts' and can be a clear unobtrusive way to switch between shots. Another common form of transition is the dissolve. This is where one clip fades into another without an abrupt cut (similar to a cross-fade in audio). In the right place, a dissolve can be used to indicate the closing of a sequence, the passing of time, or it can just indicate lazy editing! Normally, in a video you want to establish some sort of continuum, and make your shot transitions as inconspicuous as possible. By contrast, fades draw attention to the transition. This means that they need to be applied sparingly and not over-used.

Wipes

A wipe is good for covering shot transitions that might otherwise be jarring or abrupt. They occur when one element of a scene – maybe the back of someone's jacket, or a car door - completely fills the frame, allowing you to cut to a different shot without drawing attention to the transition. Although you can plan and set up wipes when you're filming, they often just happen naturally, such as when someone in a crowd walks in front of the camera.

Starting with HF4

When you first open HF4 you are shown the main home screen. This page has dynamic content and looks very much like a website - you can see that the screen shot at the beginning of this section for example, has different content to the one below. As long as you have an internet connection, it will update fairly regularly and the developers have used this as a platform for incorporating comprehensive user guides, forums and other networks.

Down the left hand side of the screen there is the shop window of downloadable add-on packs that we mentioned on page 15, and along the top, a series of tabs where you can link to various testimonials and tutorials.

Custom settings

As a general rule of thumb it is better to make your initial settings match your source material rather than your output destination. This will give you more options later on in terms of maintaining quality. So if, for example, you have some HD footage which you ultimately intend to export at a lower resolution it's usually better to edit first and reduce the resolution (i.e. quality) when you export the finished video. Enlarging low resolution video is never a good idea unless you are actually after the soggy pixilated mush that this usually produces.

Organising your files

This may seem like a fairly obvious thing to do, but it can really make a difference if you start your project with all your video and audio files, and any stills, text files or other media all stored in a separate dedicated folder – preferably on a separate hard drive on your PC, or on a high speed external drive.

Even with simple projects, things can get messy very quickly because you tend to generate lots of extra files – such as exported test clips, or bits of processed audio – that can end up being stored in random places on your C drive. Inevitably, when you find you need them later on they'll be difficult to track down.

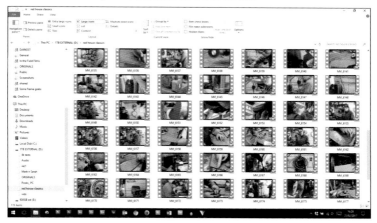

It's also useful to get into the habit of re-naming your raw video and audio files before you do anything with them. When they're recorded they're usually given a number, so re-naming with a description can make things clearer, especially when you're working with multiple files that all end up with similar numbers.

Red House Classics

For this example we're going to be working with some clips from a session with a car restorer, which was filmed in his workshop as a short promo for his website. We'll edit them to make a short sequence that shows him making a replacement panel and talking about his work. We'll use simple cuts to put the sequence together, but we'll also look at how to use a couple of useful cutting techniques - 'J cuts' and 'L cuts' which can make for smoother looking shot transitions.

Importing files

The first thing we're going to need to do is import the clips we want to use into HF4. As you can see from the file manager screenshot, a morning's filming at the workshop produced 119 video files, which is far more than we'll actually use for this sequence.

The audio was recorded straight into the camera using an external shotgun mic (see page 127), and there are also a number of separate audio files not shown in the screenshot, including a selection of wild tracks that captured noises from the different types of machinery, and general ambience recordings.

When you have a large number of clips to deal with, rather than import everything into your video editor at the start of the project, it's simpler to just go through material first in your file manager and pick out just the files that are relevant to the sequence you need to make.

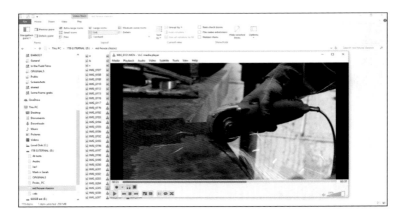

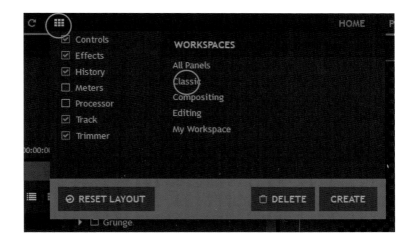

Once you have your new project open, click on **WORKSPACES.** This will bring down the various layout options. Then Click **Classic.**

This is probably the most useful pre-set workspace to start with, but you can always customise the various frames and functions to suit yourself as you become more familiar with the programme.

Selectet the **Media** tab on the left hand side menu box (next to **Controls** and **Track**), and click on **Import.** This will bring up the file manager dialogue box so you can select files to add to the project.

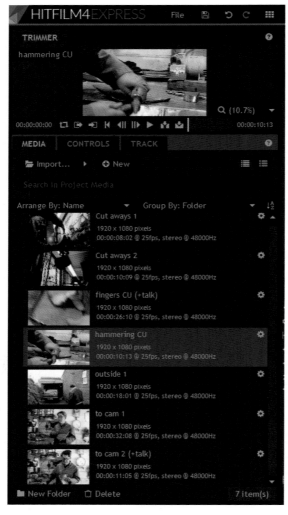

The imported clips in the media list. Seleted clips can be played in the trimmer window at the top.

For this example we've picked a varied selection of shots that relate just to the activity we're interested in. You can import as many clips as you like, but it's easier to keep track of things if you just import what you plan to use:

Two clips that include various assorted cutaways from around the workshop.

A close up shot of the restorer explaining what he's intending to do.

A close up of metal being hammered.

A generic establishing shot with the restorer walking to his work-shop.

A master shot where the restorer is explaining what he's doing

A mixed clip where the restorer talks about the work and then moves to the bench.

To begin working on the sequence, we need to select and drag clips over onto the timeline.

You can drag clips over individually, or select multiple ones. The thumbnail needs to be positioned actually on the video channel timeline (in this case Video 1)

When you're in the right place the thumbnail will outline in green and you can release your mouse. At this stage it doesn't really matter at what position along the timeline you dump the clip. When it's placed you'll see it's audio track appear.

Video track

Audio track

Splitting the audio and video

While working with your clips, the video and it's associated audio will usually be linked together, but the audio and video tracks can also be split and moved about independently. This is an important feature that we'll use at a later stage of the edit.

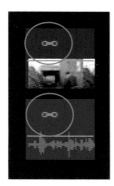 

Right clicking on a clip will open up a sub-menu, and clicking **unlink** seperates the selected video from it's associated audio. The small link symbol in the corner of a clip indictes whether or not a clip is linked. You can also re-link clips using the same right click menu.

This link / un-link function is useful if you want to replace in-camera audio for a seperate higher quality recording and need it to stay syncronised to the video while you move it around and edit it.

It's also essential if you want to use 'L 'or 'J' cuts. These involve making it so that the audio track of a clip is heard slightly before the video (a 'J cut'). An 'L-cut' on the other hand is where you see the video before you hear the audio. These types of cut are simply named after the shape they make on a timeline (see page 57).

Now we'll import the rest of the clips, and position them roughly where we want them in our sequence. The order we've chosen starts with an establishing shot of the restorer walking to his workshop, then a shot of him explaining what he's going to do, then a sub-sequence of shots (including some cutaways) of him actually working, and finally an exit shot of him holding the finished piece of work. The whole sequence will end up at around 40 seconds, and at this stage we'll just import the video files.

You can see that where the white cursor cuts the timeline relates to a particular frame of video, and this is displayed in the main viewer window.

To control the playing of video on the timeline you can use the small set of transport controls at the bottom left of the viewing window. Start and stop can also be triggered by using the space bar, but finer single frame movements backwards and forwards are also available, along with a looping function to continually repeat a selected part of the timeline. In and out markers can also be set from here.

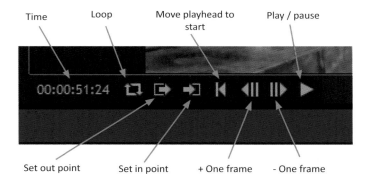

Use the scale bar at the bottom left of the timeline to zoom in and out. Set this to the left to see the whole of your project. If you drag it further to the right you can zoom down to individual frames

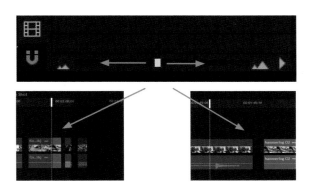

Making cuts

As it stands, the first clip on the timeline - the opening or establishing shot - works quite well as it is. It's about the correct length for what we're trying to achieve, and the camera sound that goes with the clip is fine because it's really just a low level ambient background. All we need to do to it is cut the first couple of seconds; the restorer walks into frame, then quickly out again.

We can get rid of this part of the clip in two ways. Firstly, because the part we want to remove is right at the start, we can simply shorten it by right-clicking and holding near the start of the video track, and dragging the clip start forward until it's where we want it to be.

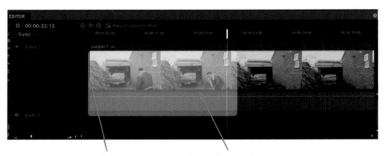

Start of clip   Part of clip to be cut

Click and hold here, and drag the edge of the clip to the right

Clip now trimmed to the right length

The other way to shorten the clip is to use the slice tool. This is the small razor icon on the toolbar to the right of the timeline.

Select the tool, then just click on the video timeline where you want to make the cut. Because the audio and video files for this clip are linked, both will be cut together and will stay linked as a new clip.

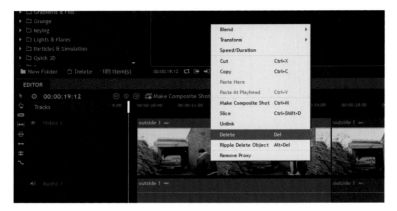

The original clip is now two seperate clips, and by right-clicking on them in the timeline you can select an options menu. Selected clips change from green to blue. In this case, as we want to get rid of the first clip, we can select **Delete.** You can also simply press the delete key to remove selected clips. If you want to keep the clip or move it to another position use the **Copy** or **Cut** commands.

Clips can also be dragged around within their own timelines or into adjacent ones by using **left-click / hold**. If you move one clip on top of another, the portion of the destination clip covered by the moved one will be overwritten.

When you've finished using the **Slice** tool, remember to re-click on the **Selection** tool to get back into normal selection mode.

Smoother transitions - using J and L cuts

Once you've got a your clips trimmed and in the order you want them, you can start connecting them together by selecting and dragging them up against one another. You can do this manually, or by using the **ripple delete** function.

Right click on the space between the clips you need to join up and select **Ripple Delete Gap.** This will shift everything to the right of the gap up to the end of the clip on the left.

It can be useful to use this function - particualry at the later stages of an edit - as it maintains the relative position of everything else in the project rather than just shifting a single clip.

Simply butting clips up against each other is a fairly rough way to edit and although you may be able to get a good visual transition, it's unlikely that any audio tracks associated with your clips will be an equally good match. You will probably find that the point at which the audio tracks join makes a noticable jump, and there may also be clicks and other distractions.

J and L cuts are great for making cuts that tie clips smoothly together and make sequences flow. Basically, a J or L cut is where you either overlap the video or audio from one clip onto the next clip. They're named after the shape they make in the editing timeline.

A J cut is where you hear the audio from the next clip before you see the video. For example, if you hear a football crowd cheering and then cut to video of a match, that would be a J Cut.

We'll use a J cut to make the transition between the first two clips in our sequence smoother. You can see that the audio on the first clip is just quiet background noise, whereas the talking on the second clip comes in abruptly right at the cut.

To make a J cut between these two clips we first need to unlink the audio and video on the clips by clicking on the small chain symbols. Do this seperately for each clip.

Now, if we click on the audio track of the first clip, it should become highlighted blue. Putting the cursor at the far right edge of the audio **click / hold** allows us to drag the edge of the track towards the left, effectively creating a couple of seconds silence on the timeline at the end of the clip. Do the same to the far left of the video track

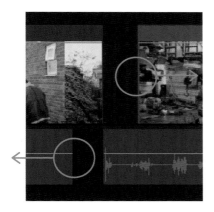

Be careful not to move any of the audio or video tracks or they will be out of sync. If you find you've done this later on in the edit it can be a nightmare to line things up again.

Next, select the gap between two of the tracks and right click **Ripple Delete.**

This will bring the two clips together, but there will probably still be a small gap between either the audio or the video. Use the edge selection techneque to close this up and then re-link the audio and video tracks by selecting a video / audio pair, right clicking on the time-line and selecting **Re-link.** An L cut can be done in the same way but will have the video cut in front of the audio.

A J cut

An L cut

Refining an audio transition

Cuts in your audio track will rarely sound smooth and unobtrusive if you leave them as they are. Even if the clips you are cutting were recorded in the same session the shifts from one to the other will often be quite noticable - particulalry on headphones.

One way to get round this is to use a **crossfade** so that the audio from one clip gradually fades out while the next one fades in. This can be done by using the **Fade** effect from the **Effects** menu.

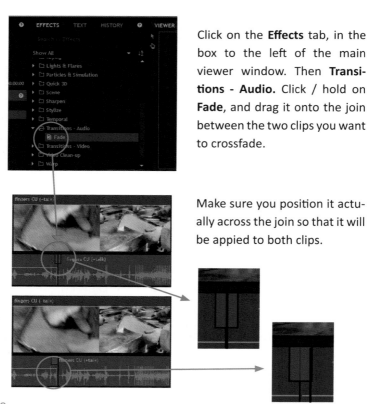

Click on the **Effects** tab, in the box to the left of the main viewer window. Then **Transitions - Audio.** Click / hold on **Fade**, and drag it onto the join between the two clips you want to crossfade.

Make sure you position it actually across the join so that it will be appied to both clips.

If you place the transition to the left or right of the junction, a normal fade-out or fade-in will be applied to the clip it's positioned on, rather than a cross-fade between the two. You can change the duration of the fade or cross-fade by click / holding on the edge of the blue box and dragging it along the timeline.

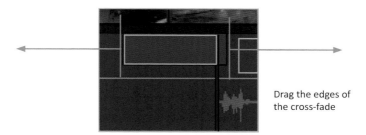

Drag the edges of the cross-fade

A more advanced way of applying fades is to use **keyframes**. These can be added to the audio and video timelines to control effects and other processes. To create a cross-fade using keyframes you will need to have the audio for the two clips you want to mix on different tracks. Do this by right clicking on an existing audio track and selecting **Insert Track**.

Inserting a new audio track

A new audio track will appear under the existing one, and a new empty video track above the existing video. Next, keeping the audio and video linked for now, drag the audio from one clip down onto the new track. As you do this the video clip will move up onto to its new track as well.

Now either click **Unlink** on this clip and drag the left hand edge of the audio so it extends under the first clip. Or, if you are right at the start of a clip and there is no 'hidden' audio to expose, keep the audio and video tacks linked and drag both to the left so that there is an overlap

Drag the audio onto a new track

Drag the audio to overlap the tracks

Applying keyframes

To create a simple audio fade-out on the first clip, and a corresponding fade-in on the second, we need to put keyframes on the audio level line. This is the white line that runs the length of each clip. Dragging it up or down sets the volume level, and putting keyframes on it allows you to control this very precisely.

Audio keyframes are applied by holding down **ctrl** and clicking on the volume level line. Re-clicking allows you to delete any keyframes you don't need, and they can also be dragged around along the line.

Once you've placed the keyframes you need - in this case four of them - you can click / hold on the end ones in each clip and drag them down to the bottom of the timeline. This will set the volume level at these points to zero. The two other keyframes in this crossfade act as anchor points for the fade. Keyframes can be used to control most other effects and processes that you might want to apply to a video or audio clip.

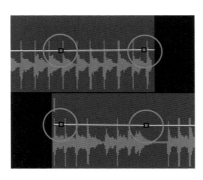

Keyframes on the volume control line

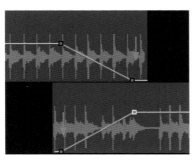

A cross-fade using keyframes

Applying transitions to video clips

Creating a dissolve between two clips in HF4 is relatively easy. Here, we'll put a disolve betwee two clips. First, from the **Effects** menu select **Transitions**, **Disolve**, **Cross Disolve**. Then click and drag this over to the point where the two clips join. The clips must be right up against each other (**Ripple Delete** will make sure they are). A blue box will appear across the joint marking where the fade will be. This is at a default length, but can be changed by hovering your mouse over the edges. The mouse pointer will turn into a blue bracket symbol, and you can click and drag this along the timeline to make a longer transition

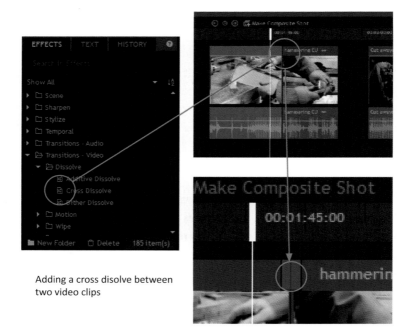

Adding a cross disolve between two video clips

4 Making a gaming video

Gaming videos are hugely popular on YouTube, with every major game having its own sub-culture of enthusiasts who regularly upload hours of footage. Often this is simply live gameplay recorded with a capture card and uploaded. There may be some additional audio such as a running commentary, but usually there's very little in the way of editing or post-production.

What we'll look at in this section is how to produce a live gameplay video that's a bit more refined. We'll use one of the freely available screen capture utilities to record everything that happens on-screen. And we'll video our gamer as he plays, while also recording his live commentary.

We'll then we'll use Hit Film 4 to edit the footage, syncronise the gameplay and player tracks and create an on-screen insert so that we can also see what the player is doing and saying as he plays. Finally we'll look at exporting the finished video in a format suitable for uploading to YouTube.

Video capture
There are quite a few options if you want to record what's happening on your computer screen or games console. The latest consoles such as the PlayStation 4, Playstion 4 Pro, Xbox One, Xbox One S and Wii U all have features which allow you to take shots of the screen, record live action and make live streams. These HD recordings can then simply be uploaded directly to YouTube as they are, or to your video editor.

Elgato game capture HD60

If you're using your PC or an older console, or just want a bit more versatility, you can use a game capture device which records via the HDMI output. These usually connect between your device and your TV (or your PC and your monitor). Internal PC capture cards are also available.

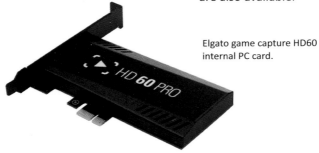

Elgato game capture HD60 internal PC card.

A third option if you're using a PC is to download a screen recording utility such as **Bandicam**. Don't be tempted to try and video your PC screen as the quality will be awful.

For this gaming video we'll be using Bandicam to record our live gameplay. This application is very popular with gamers because it's easy to use, very stable and can save your capture files in AVI or MP4 video formats. It'll also capture screen grabs and save them as BMP, PNG or JPG image files. The free version is limited to 10 minutes record time and puts a (fairly unobtrusive) watermark on the top of the video. The full download isn't expensive though, has unlimited record time and no watermark.

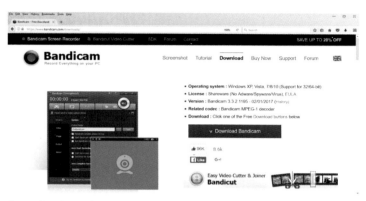

Download Bandicam at:

https://www.bandicam.com/downloads/

User forum at:

https://forum.bandicam.com/

Setting up Bandicam

Once you've downloaded Bandicam, the initial setup for game recording is very straightforward.

When you open the pro-gramme for the first time you'll get this main screen. Make sure you're in game record mode (the far left tab with the game controller on it). In the general settings menu set your output folder to wherever it is you are storing your video files.

If you want to have your FPS (frames per second) rate displayed on screen during your recordings, click on show **FPS Overlay** on the FPS tab. You can also enable F9 as a hotkey to toggle this on and off.

In the **Video** settings menu you can change the primary sound device and select various other options such as adding a logo to your recording.

Use the **Format** setting menu to set the resolution and format of your output file.

As we are going to video the gamer as he plays, and then synchronise this to the screen recording, we need a set-up that will enable us to get a good quality continuous shot of him in front of his monitor. We're also going to use an external mic positioned in front of him to record his live commentary.

It would be fine to take an audio feed from the microphone in his gaming headset, but the quality is likely to be a bit rough, and any-way, in this genre of video it looks cooler to have the mic and pop shield in shot.

Bandicam has a function that allows you to record from the camera on your PC or laptop. but for a much more versatile set-up we're going to use a DSLR on a tripod to one side of the gamer, behind his monitor. This won't be moved during the video so it's said to be 'locked off'. We've got a single large soft light behind the monitor, pointing face on to the the gamer, and a neutral backdrop.

We've not directly lit the backdrop as the ambient light in the room was giving a fairly even effect over the small area that was visible.

For recording the audio, we're going to use a condenser mic on a suspension boom stand. This one is a fairly typical 'budget' model and doesn't have any kind of mechanical isolation. So if you're using one of these mounted on a desk you need to be careful or it will pick up any knocks and other mechanical noise.

As an alternative you could use a conventional boom mic stand, which because it'll be standing on the floor, should give a higher level of mechanical isolation. This type of stand isn't as convenient though, and tends not to be used as much for this kind of video.

In front of the mic we've got a pop shield which is there to limit the pops and bumps produced by 'plosive' sounds, such as words that start with the letter 'B' or 'P'. A pop shield is really just a bit of nylon mesh on a frame that disrupts the force of the air expelled during these sounds before it gets to the mic.

The recording of the live commen-try will be done on a digital re-corder. In this case the mic will be going through a small mixer before it reaches the recorder, but this is really just so we can use it to supply phantom power. If your camera has an external mic input you could plug directly into that, but as we mention in the audio section, camera audio can be a bit patchy, even with a good camera and an external mic.

Some gamers make a feature of the rough headphone mic sound, and if you're recording a multi-player online game you'll probably want to capture the low-res audio coming from all of the the other player's headsets. In these situations it's most straightforward to just use the game capture audio.

In this case, the audio from the game itself will be recorded as the audio track of the video capture file, and as you ideally need to keep the gamer's live recording free of any in-game sound, the gamer will be using headphones rather than speakers when actually recording. Again, this is all part of the 'look' of this type of video. If you don't want to show the headphones, you could just use an unobtrusive ear-phone as a monitor.

Recording the video

Once you're set up and ready to go, it's just a question of synchronising the video, audio and gameplay recordings. Unlike other settings where you can just clap your hands to create a transient spike that's picked up on the camera and external mic, here we also need to create some kind of peak marker to help synchronise the gameplay audio. You may be able to set your screen capture device to record a few seconds of headphone commentary and then switch over to game sounds only, but this might be awkward to arrange.

Another option is to set everything going (i.e. the video, external audio recorder, the game, and the screen recorder) then put your headphones near the external mic and play a few seconds of game audio – the clicking noises that often go with menu selection make good transients. Isolated or loud percussive sounds will show up clearly on the audio timelines when you come to synchronise things later.

It will pay to do a couple of trial runs before you make a final recording. Check that your framing is ok, and be aware of how far you can move without going out of shot. Ideally you should be able to see the monitor screen of your camera, but this isn't always possible.

Make sure your external audio recording levels are ok, and be familiar with how your screen recorder works. Faffing about a bit at the start of the reocording doesn't really matter because it can all be edited out, but it's obviulsly better to be clear about what you're doing.

When you're finally ready to play, get the game to the point that you intend to record from, take a few seconds pause and just let the equipment run. This will make a useful marker on the various time-lines to indicate the start of the proper recording and make it easier to edit together a smooth opening.

If you're intending to do some sort of introduction, you can do it live at this point, and then move into the gameplay. If you're only going to record a voice-over (i.e. if you're not filming the insert) it doesn't matter when you do your voice recording - you could even record parts of it later while watching a playback of your screen capture, although this will loose some of the 'liveness'.

When you've finished your gameplay, you might also want to record some sort of sign-off. Particulalry if this is to be one of a regular series of uploads.

Putting it together

You'll now have at least a couple of video files (the screen capture file and the live comentary video file). You'll also have your live commentary audio if you recorded this on a seperate device. Put these into a new folder and re-name them.

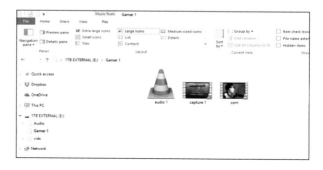

We'll use Hit Film 4 to edit our video. So we'll open up a new project and import the files.

Synchronising external audio

Before we can start to edit, we need to synchronise the audio from the external mic, the audio from the game capture and the audio from the camera. We'll start with the camera and external audio tracks because the audio waveforms on these should be very similar and relatively easy to line up. This process can be used to sync any camera and external audio files.

Drag the two files from the Media window onto the timeline and roughly line them up so that they are one on top of the other.

Re-size the audio track view so that you can clearly see both waveforms of the two tracks. Do this by clicking on the small triangle to the right of the timeline Scale bar. This will bring up a menu with the audio, video and preview sizing options. Set the audio timeline to **Large**.

Timeline scale bar menu

Now you can synchronise the tracks. Do this by finding a large peak that shows up clearly on both tracks, then shift one of the tracks by clicking and dragging it until the waveforms are as close as you can get them. Make sure the snap function is disabled (the small magnet shaped icon to the left of the increment scale). Then expand the audio tracks so you can line the waveforms up really accurately. Keep checking the audio while you do this. When you're close you will begin to hear what sounds like a short echo. This will become shorter and more metalic the nearer you get to an accurate sync. The closer you can zoom in to the audio, the more accurate you will be able to be.

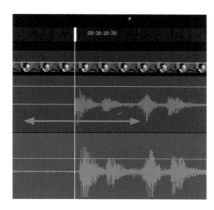

Use the white cursor line to help you match up the tracks

When the two tracks are lined up you can mute the camera audio by clicking on the small speaker icon to the left of the track name label, or strip it out completely by unlinking it from its video track and deleting it. Make sure you then link the external audio to the video before you do anything else so that everything stays synced.

Finally, you can import your game capture file. Put it onto a track below the live video, and synchronise it with the commentary audio. This might be more tricky unless you've recorded some of the game sound as a reference to line things up, but totally accurate sync may not be vital for this track. Here are all of the tracks in position on the timeline.

You can see that we've deleted the original camera audio and replaced it with the externally recorded track, and there are two video tracks - the game capture and the live comentary. Because the commentary video is on the uppermost video track, it is effec-

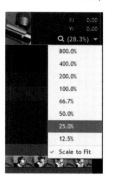

tively 'on top' of the game play in the monitor window. So what we want to do now is re-size the commentary video so that it's displayed as a small box in one corner of the screen.

To do this, first set the monitor window to a size that allows you to see the entire outline of the frame using the drop down menu to the bottom right of the display.

Then click on the picture in the window and a blue box will appear around it.

Use your mouse to drag the corners of this box to the size and position you want, relative to the game play frame, which you'll now be able to see behind.

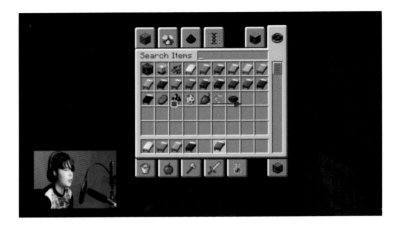

The finished layout should look something like this, with the recording of the game play as the main element and the synchronised live commentary superimposed on top. You can of course make the insert any size you like.

The last thing to do before exporting is to tidy up the start and finish. In this case we're simply going to apply transitions so that the game footage and audio fade in smoothly, followed a few seconds later by the commentary. Then, as the game play gets underway, we'll fade in the commentary insert video.

With the beginning of the video cut so that it starts at a point just before the actual game play gets underway, and all of the transitions in place, the screen shots on the next page show what the timeline ends up like. Remember that to change the length of the video and associated audio tracks seperately, you need to **unlink** them (see page 56).

Game play video fades in   Commentary video fades in

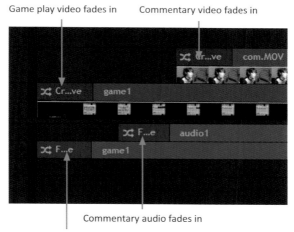

Commentary audio fades in

Game play audio fades in

Game play video fades out

Commentary video fades out

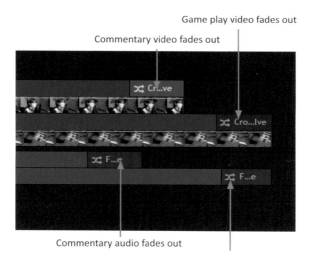

Commentary audio fades out

Game play audio fades out

Exporting video

Assuming you are going to export your video in a format that'll work well on a platform like YouTube, there's just the question of which export settings to use to maintain the best quality.

Luckily, many video editing packages now have pre-sets you can use. HF4 is particularly useful in this respect because it not only has a YouTube pre-set, but if you have a channel already, and an internet connection it can render and upload a video straight to your account. Simply click on the **Export** tab at the top of the screen (next to **Edit**) and select **YouTube**.

5 Sound recording and production

Choosing audio production software

Most decent video editing packages have fairly extensive audio functionality built in, and this will let you do most audio production without having to use a separate programme. But in practice, apart from simple cuts and trimming, it's often useful to be able to prepare your audio using an external audio editor at a particular point in the production process – i.e. when all the video elements are pretty much where you want them.

DAW software running on a Mac

An audio software production environment is usually called a 'Digital Audio Workstation' or DAW, and is basically a dedicated piece of equipment or software that can be used for recording, editing and producing audio files. These can be anything from songs and pieces of music, through to speech and sound effects.

Regardless of complexity, a DAW will have a central interface that allows you to either work on and edit single audio files – performing functions such as trimming, fading, noise reduction, applying effects and so on – or to mix multiple files (tracks) together into a final produced piece.

For the audio examples in this book we've chosen to use a programme called **Audacity**. This is full function, open source audio editing software for PC and Mac that stands up really well against much more expensive professional production packages.

Audacity basically developed as a simple audio editing utility, but has undergone a long process of incremental improvement. It's currently able to do both single file editing and multi-track work, which begins to define it more as a fully-fledged DAW rather than simply a file editor.

Audacity is widely used as a recommended download in schools and colleges, and as with many open source programmes it has a vibrant community of users and developers.

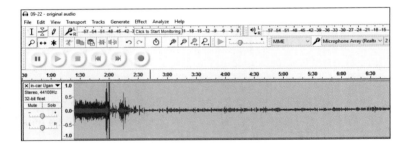

The 'official' Audacity forum is at:
http://forum.audacityteam.org/

Other choices

Along with Audacity, there are loads of othr widely used and relatively inexpensive (even free) packages that can take you all the way
to a professional level in terms of functionality and output quality.

Most of the more professional ones use a relatively similar interface,
so once you're familiar with the kinds of tasks you need an audio
editor for it's not too hard to switch from one to another.

We've listed a few other popular programmes here. The list was put
together with the emphasis on software that's reasonably accessible
to a relative beginner, but which will still hold up as levels of exper-
tise and the corresponding demand for more advanced functions
increases.

As you'll see if you check out any of the download links, with a lot
of the more serious audio production software tending to be used
by musicians, there's a slight differentiation between packages that
are focused purely on studio based production (Reaper, for example),
and those which are optimised for live performance such as Ableton
Live. These packages can be used for live control of electronic instruments as well as offline audio and are specifically designed to be fully
functioning DAWs rather than just audio editors.

Most of these programmes, for example, provide easy integration
with MIDI (or musical instrument digital interface) which is the standard protocol for digital communication between computers, external
(music) keyboards, samplers and virtually any other piece of electronic music hardware.

Access to VST (virtual studio technology) instruments and other
performance-specific features are also fairly standard, although
the more performance oriented software may include specialised
features such as live pre-sets that make controlling VST instruments
and effects easier during live performance. Any of these programmes
will easily handle the basic production we are concerned with, so
what might be of more concern are issues of cost and ease of use.

Ableton Live 9

Since its introduction in 1999, Ableton Live has been a very popular DAW. It comes with huge sound libraries and very comprehensive
MIDI implementation, which makes it great for live performance as
well as production. A less expensive 'starter' version is also available.

Download Ableton Live at:
http://www.ableton.com

Image-Line Fruity Loops

Like Ableton Live, Fruity Loops has been around for quite a while and has an interface which is especially well-suited to beginners. It's another good choice for starting out in audio production.

Download Fruity Loops at:
http://www.image-line.com/downloads/flstudiodownload.html

User forum:
http://forum.image-line.com/

Apple Logic Pro X

If you use a Mac, this is a really well featured package. A step up from the hugely popular (and free) Garage Band, it's not exactly for the beginner, but with its relatively intuitive user interface, it's worth spending the time to learn it.

Download Apple Logic Pro X at:

https://itunes.apple.com/us/app/logic-pro-x/id634148309

User forums:

https://www.logicprohelp.com/forum/

Propellerhead Reason

Propellerhead Reason is aimed slightly above beginner level and is a powerful mid-range DAW.

Download Reason at:

https://www.propellerheads.se/download/

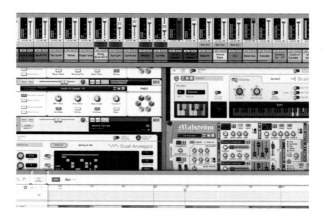

Steinberg Cubase

Cubase has one of the biggest sound libraries that come bundled with any DAW, and has a strong following. It's recommended for more experienced users.

If you use an iPad, there's also a limited function app available 'Cubasis' that's designed to integrate easily with the main programme and is good for sketching out ideas or recording and exporting audio.

Download Cubase at:

https://www.steinberg.net/en/products/steinberg_trial_versions.html

Cockos Reaper

Like Audacity, Reaper is open-source software coded by a small group of dedicated enthusiasts. Powerful and easy to use, you can download a fully functional version of this programme free for 60 days, then pay for a (very inexpensive) licence to carry on using it.

Download Reaper at:

http://www.reaper.fm/download.php

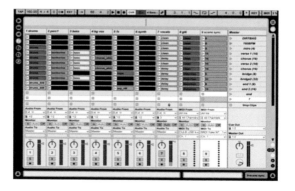

Getting started with Audacity

Setting up the programme

As always with free and open source software, it's best to download direct from the developer rather than any of the dubious sites that will inevitably crop up if you just type 'audacity' into Google. The genuine **Audacity** developer's site is at: http://www.audacityteam.org/

Clicking on that link will take you to the downloads page:

Click on the green download Audacity link, then select the version you want from the next screen.

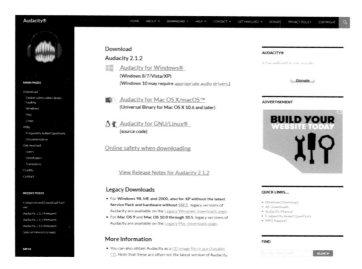

This opens up a dialogue box. Click on save file, and follow the rest of the download process as normal. Audacity is a relatively small file, so the download and set-up should only take a couple of minutes.

When you open Audacity for the first time you'll see the main work screen. Most of the controls are in the bar across the top and the workspace - where the files you want to work with are displayed - is the big grey area in the middle. At start-up, this area will be empty.

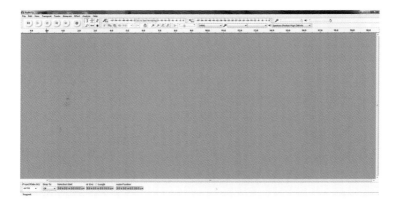

You can simply use Audacity to work on single audio files exported from your video editor (to apply noise reduction, for example), and we'll look at how to do this later in the chapter.

However, there's a lot more that the software can do, including multi-track work. As a DAW, Audacity can work with as many tracks as your hardware can handle, which opens up endless creative possibilities in terms of sound design. Individual tracks can be manipulated independently and positioned in relation to one another.

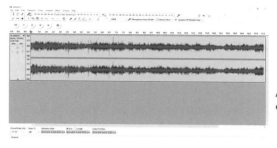

Audacity being used to edit a single audio file.

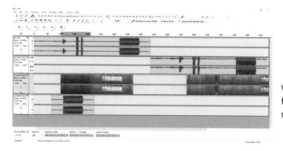

Working with several files in multi-track mode.

Basic functions

Let's take a look at how Audacity is laid out, and where to find some of the main functions. The coloured buttons along the left of the main toolbar are the transport controls, which can be used for starting and stopping playback of the audio file you are working on. The purple double arrows allow you to scrub back to the start or end of a file quickly, and the red button on the right is the record switch.

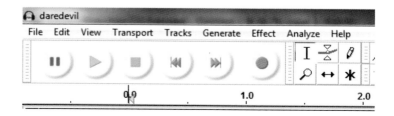

The space bar on your keyboard can also be used to start and stop the audio playback, and in practice this is usually more convenient than using the mouse.

Along the top are the usual drop-down menus. **File** has all the saving, importing and exporting options.

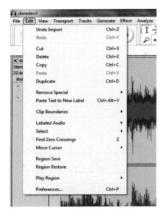

The **Edit** menu is where you'll find the basic cut and paste functions, as well as many more sophisticated tools for working with regions of audio within a file

The **View** menu has options for sizing the waveform display and zooming it in and out, as well as the list of toolbars that are available for display in the work-space. Most of these are open as default on start-up, but they can be turned off as required if the workspace is getting crowded.

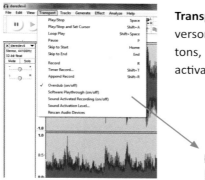

Transport has the menu accessed versons of the main transport buttons, as well as overdub and sound activated record settings.

The **Tracks** menu allows you to select and work with various track functions such as mute and sync-lock.

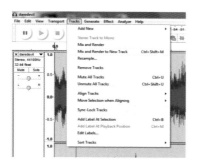

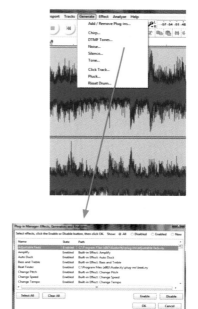

Generate brings up a list of fairly random effects sounds including a tone generator and a white noise source. It can also be used to add or remove third party VST (virtual studio technology) effects.

All of the effects that come bundled with the programme (such as equalisers (EQ), filters and delays), and any third-party ones that you may have downloaded end up listed in the **Effects** menu, and there are some interesting tools in **Analyse**, including a sound finder and various frequency plotting devices.

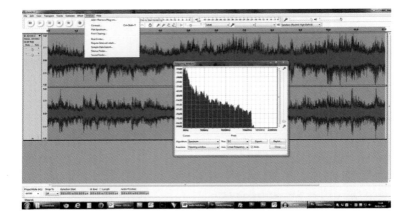

A lot of the functions in the dropdown menus are also accessible directly from customisable toolbars. These are arranged in groups of related functions.

So for example, the sub-group for controlling the microphone inputs are in one group, and the editing tools are in a separate group. All of these sub-groups can be dragged about independently to anywhere on the screen using the patterned rectangles at the end of each tool-bar. They can also be removed completely by using the toolbars control in the View menu.

Working with sound files

In this section, we're going to look at how to use Audacity to do some simple editing and cleaning up of a sound file. We'll also show you how to apply some processing and export the finished audio back into your video editor.

We're going to use a wild track file from the demonstration video in chapter 3 as an example because this is a simple stand-alone file, and we can mess about with it without having to worry about re-synchronising it to a particular piece of video when it's imported into our video editor.

Importing audio

First open Audacity, click on File then Open, and find the directory you're using to store your audio files. In this case we're storing our video and audio files in the same directory, and we're after a file called 'Wild2', at the bottom of the list.

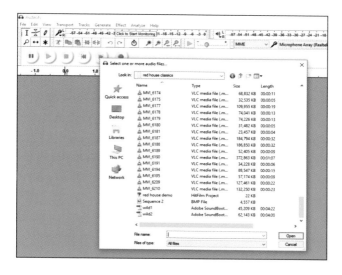

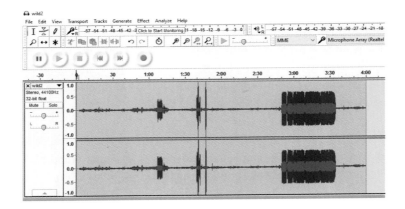

The imported audio looks like this. It's a four minute file with quite a lot of variation in the sounds that were captured. The time in minutes and seconds is shown across the top of the timeline. The recording was made on a digital recorder using built-in stereo condenser mics, so the left and right channel are displayed together. You can split the two channels and work on them seperately, but to start with we'll treat them as a single file.

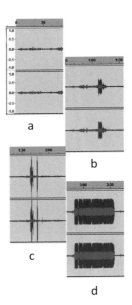

The first minute or so (a) is just general workshop ambiance - the restorer moving bits of equipment around, setting up tools, some fragments of talking etc. Then at around 1m15s there is the sound of a compressor being started up and shut off (b), followed at 1m40s by some hammering (c). The section from around 1m45s to 2m45s is more general ambiance, followed by the sound of an angle grinder being used (d).

The first thing we're going to do is make a separate file that just has 20 or so seconds of 'general ambiance'. This will be only low key background sound with no loud or distracting noises such as the angle grinder. In order to do this we'll first find the part of the file that we want to keep. This is roughly the period from 1m50s to 2m45s.

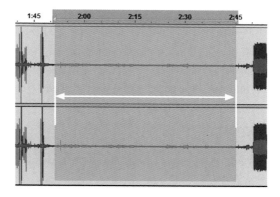

To select a part of the file, click and hold down near the centre of the timeline and drag the cursor along. While it's in the right area for selection, the cursor icon will have an I-beam shape. if you move outside of the timeline it will revert back to a normal arrow shape, if you move onto the ruler area at the top of the timeline it changes to a hand symbol and this is used to shift the play cursor along the file.

Next, click on **Edit, Copy**. Then make a new empty file by clicking **File, New.** This opens up a new window into which you can paste your coppied selection with **Edit, Paste**.

 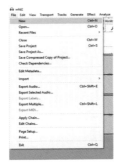 

As it currently stands, Audacity will open a whole new instance of itself every time you create a new file, which can be annoying, but all of your other files remain open and can be accessed if you hover over the programme icon on the taskbar at the bottom of the screen:

It's always a good idea to make a copy of any files you want to use before you start editing, and work on those rather than your originals.

Any actions you perform in Audacity can be undone using the **Undo** and **Redo** buttons or **ctrl-Z** on the keyboard, but if you actually save any changes you'll overwrite the original file and won't be able to go back and adjust things.

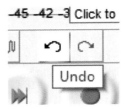

The new file looks like this:

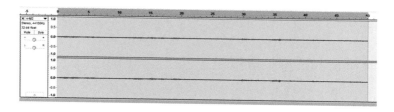

You can see that we just have 50 seconds or so of background ambience. Because this is basically quite low level sound, the waveform isn't that easy to see. We can improve the view by zooming the verticle axis. This won't change the level of the sound, just the view of it on the timeline.

To zoom in and out horizontally, hold down **ctrl** and use your **scroll wheel**. For vertical zooming, it's the same, but you need to put your cursor on the vertical scale - it will change into a small magnifying glass when you're in the right place.

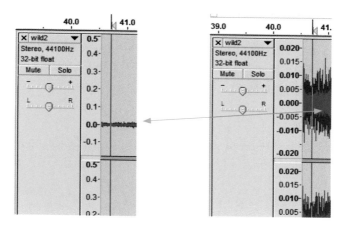

With an expanded vertical scale the waveform is easier to see:

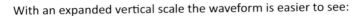

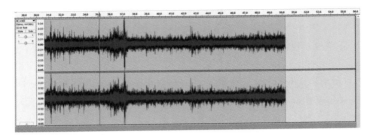

Now it needs to be saved as a new file. Click **File**, **Export**, and save it under a new name in the directory that you're using for your other working files. In the **Save as type** box below where you put the new file name, choose **16 or 32 bit WAV** unless you particulalry need one of the compressed file types.

The saved file can now be given some more processing (see next section) or simply imported into your video editor. On the **File** menu there is also an option to **Save**, but this will only save your Audacity project and won't export your file.

Useful effects

To keep things straightforward, most of the essential tasks you'll want
to perform on your audio are probably easiest to do using the audio
functions in your video production package.

This might include applying transitions (i.e. fading sections of audio in
or out); adjusting the relative volume levels of tracks in response to
the action (i.e. dropping the level of a background or wild track during a voice over), or applying basic equalisation (EQ). Any half decent
video editing application will give you this level of functionality.

For simple projects such as the gaming video, that will only have
one or two separate audio tracks to deal with, and won't really need
much in the way of effects or processing, this will often be much less
trouble than trying to export random fragments of audio and shift
them around between programmes. You'll run into fewer of the syn-
chronisation issues and other gremlins that will inevitably crop up.

Where using an external programme like Audacity can be really effective though is for:

1) Pre-processing your audio before you import it into your video
editor so that any effects that need to be applied to the whole file -
such as noise reduction - will be uniform.

2) Processing the audio from your completed production (i.e. once
you're happy you've got a balanced edit, export the audio as a single
file, tighten up the production and re-import import it.)

Normalisation

You can use normalisation to set the peak amplitude of a piece of audio. Basically, it's useful for making quiet tracks louder without affecting their dynamic properties, as you would if you applied other processes such as compression.

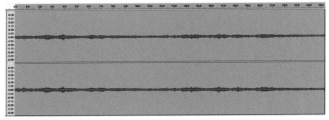

Original wild track

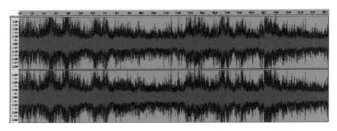

After normalisation

Here you can see the effect of normalisation on the wild track file we made in the last section. You can see that this is not simply zoomed in because the vertical scale range is the same in both cases.

To apply normalisation to an audio file, simply click on **Effects** in the menu at the top of the screen, then select **Normalise**. This will apply the effect to the whole file by default, although you can also just apply it to selected sections.

Noise reduction

The noise reduction processing available in Audacity is fairly basic but with a little trial and error can produce some great results. For this example we'll use the audio track from a video clip that was recorded on a cheap DSLR using an external mic. Because the microphone was reasonably good, the audio was usable. However, the camera electronics introduced a high level of background hiss, and this needs to be removed.

Hiss removal is one of the more straightforward noise reduction tasks and one that often has a pre-set of its own. Audacity uses a system which samples a section of the noise you want to remove, and then basically subtracts this from the main file. It's a system that can work well, but depends a lot on the sample of 'noise' you can provide for the algorithm to work with. The noise reduction tab is in the **Effects** menu. Before using it, you need to select a part of your file where there is nothing other than the noise that you want to remove. (i.e. in this case the hiss).

Here, there's a good couple of seconds where the interviewee isn't talking and there's little other than background hiss from the cheap camera pre-amp. This part needs to be selected making sure none of the talking at either side is included as this will confuse the system.

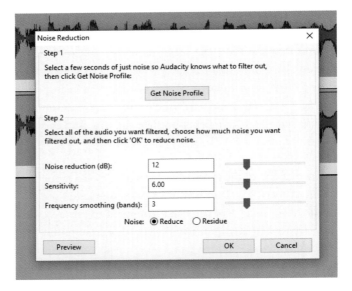

When you open up **Noise Reduction** you'll get a dialogue box with an option to **Get Noise Profile.** Click this and it'll use the selection you've just made as it's profile. It'll carry on using this until you choose another one, so it's important to sample a fresh noise profile when you start on a new file.

You will then need to select the part of the file you want to process (**ctrl + A** to select the whole file). In order to get the best results, click **Preview** and tweak the sliders on the right hand side.

When you're satisfied that you've got the best compromise between the noise reduction and colouring of the sound, click **OK**, wait for the processing to finish and save the file under a new name. Don't save it with the same name because you won't be able to undo your changes and they will overwrite your original file.

Mono to stereo

If you're making recordings with an external mic, these will often be in mono. If you use them in a video without converting them to stereo they'll end up coming out of just one speaker, or more distract-ingly, one side of a pair of headphones.

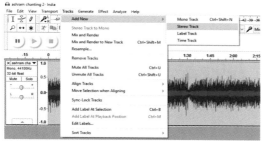

To convert a mono track to stereo, first open your mono track. Then select **Tracks**, **New**, **Stereo track**.

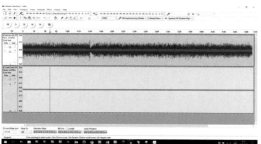

Click on the mono timeline and **ctrl + A** to select the whole file, then **Edit**, **Cut**.

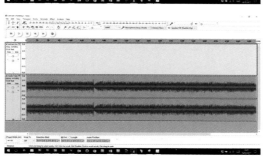

Click on the stereo timeline and **Edit**, **Paste**. This will copy the mono track onto both stereo tracks

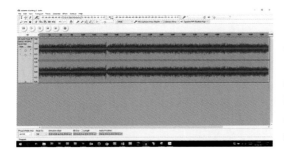

Finally, remove the old mono track by clicking on the small X in the top left hand corner of its timeline and save the file.

Equalisation

Equalization (EQ) is basically just a form of advanced tone control. It's a way of manipulating sounds by their frequency, and allows you to increase the level of some frequencies and reduce others. EQ in Audacity is accessed from the **Effects** menu. You can apply various simple pre-sets, such as the 100Hz rumble filter that's shown on the next page, using **Select curve**. There are also a couple of treble and bass boosters, and some novelty effects like 'telephone' and 'walky talky'.

The Audacity EQ has two modes: **Graphic EQ** and **Draw curves**. These are selected with the **EQ type** buttons below the frequency response graph. The graphic mode has sliders for different frequency bands – higher frequencies to the right and lower frequencies to the left, and these are common to both modes. If you go into draw mode you can drag the frequency curve around and set points wherever you want them.

To apply EQ to a file, select the part you want to work on, then from the upper toolbar: **Effect, Equalisation**. You can use **Preview** to hear the effect your changes are making before you commit. EQ is best used sparingly.

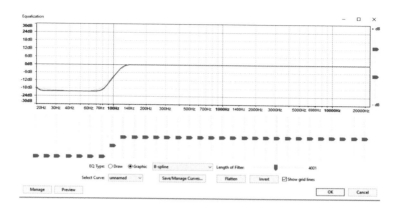

Graphic mode. The blue sliders cut or boost frequency bands

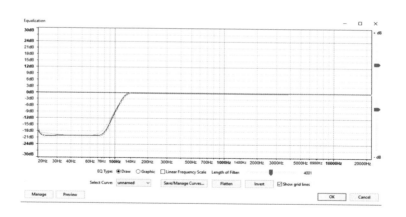

Draw curves mode. Click on the line of the graph to place anchor points and drag them to where you want them.

6 Recording sound for video

External microphones

Most camcorders, smartphones and DSLRs are very limited when it comes to the quality of sound given by their built-in microphones. No matter how well designed their microphones are, or how good the audio processing is in the camera, building a microphone in will always result in a lot of compromises – mostly at the expense of audio quality.

Probably the most serious of these is the picking up of unwanted mechanical sounds from the case of whatever it is you're using – the sound of your fingers rubbing on the plastic, the buzzing of the autofocus, or the clicks you make when you change a switch setting. All of this gets transmitted through the body of the camera and picked up by the mic. It can ruin what might otherwise be usable audio.

The other big drawback of using an internal mic is that you are unlikely to have much useful control over how you use it. A lot of camcorders and DSLRs – even fairly expensive professional models - will just have a couple of mics stuck in the front of the case. If you're lucky you may have some degree of manual control over the input levels for these, but there's unlikely to be an actual physical control. Electronic control will be buried somewhere in an audio settings menu, which makes adjusting levels on the go awkward. More commonly there will simply be a pre-set automatic level control. The video / audio settings on a smartphone will be just as limiting.

Making good recordings

Here are some things you might consider when recording sound for video. We'll assume that you'll be able to use some sort of external microphone, and hopefully an external digital recorder recorder as well (see later on).

Close mic

Try to get your mic as close as possible to whatever it is you are recording. This highlights another drawback of using a camera's built in microphone - it will rarely be close enough for good results - particularly if you're trying to capture dialogue or recording interviews. A good option for these situations can be a lapel or lavalier (small hands-free) mic. Wireless versions of these are particulalry useful, especially if your subject is likely to move about.

If you're recording something like a live band, take advantage of the sound equipment that's already likely to be there. If there's a PA system and a sound engineer, see if you can take a line out from the mixing desk and record that (don't try this at big gigs unless you've arranged it beforehand!).

If you've able to do a proper set-up, Individual instruments and amplifiers can have their own mics or lineout and you can take everything to a mixer. The camera sound can then be syncronised and replaced with the proper recording when you come to edit.

Check the location

If you can, visit the place where you will be recording and check for potential problems - noisy air conditioning, people moving around, slamming doors, traffic noise etc. You may not be able to do much about many of these, but you might be able to make contingency plans - maybe even change location.

Monitoring

If you can, always monitor your sound on headphones. This doesn't really apply to smartphones or basic camcorders, but for decent sound it's essential to be able to hear what you're recording live. Simply checking the levels on a camera's VU meters will only tell you the level of your recording. It won't tell you whether or not there's too much background noise.

Wind noise

If you're recording outside, cut down on wind noise with a mic cover such as the ubiquitous 'dead cat' (see next page). These can be really effective even in quite extreme conditions. They work by breaking up air turbulence before it gets to the microphone element while remaining acoustically transparent. As with live cats though, they're not very effective if they get wet.

Artificial fur wind shields make a huge difference when compared to standard foam ones and you can also get them to use with the built in mics on most digital recorders. At a push, you can simply put your recorder inside a fur mic wind shield and use it as a sort of wind proof bag. The drawback with this is that you can't easily get to the controls, and rustlings created by movement of the fabric liner on the mics can be just as troublesome. But it's fine if you are leaving the recorder in place for a while – such as at an open-air concert.

If you like to experiment, it's easy to make your own wind shield. Although there's a lot of nerdy debate over just how effective different types of fake fur actually are. This DIY dead cat was made out of a piece of coat collar trim. It works fine. It's best to try and get

material that's as close in texture and strand length as commercially available shields, and has a base fabric that's as thin as possible, but virtually any long fake fur enclosing the mic should break up the air and make some improvement. Real fur, such as an old mink stole probably won't work too well because the leather backing will tend to block too much high frequency sound.

Digital audio recorders

Although it is usually possible to connect an external mic to a DSLR or camcorder, and this can be a fantastic improvement over the performance of an internal mic, the facilities for controlling the recording are still often very limited. Issues such as inability to monitor live sound, having to make do with pre-set input levels, and awful signal-to-noise performance (usually in the form of background hiss) are going to crop up – even if you use a really good microphone. It's better to think of your audio as something completely separate from your video, and use a digital audio recorder (or even a smartphone, as we'll see in the next section) to record your sound.

Roland R-05

Zoom H4N

Tascam DR-40

Three mid-range digital audio recorders. Any of these will produce fantastic results if you use them correctly. As is fairly standard now, they all have high quality stereo condenser mics mounted on the top, which can be useful for ambient recordings, and they use SD cards for storing their files. The Zoom and Tascam models pictured here also have XLR inputs for taking professional mics, and can provide phantom power. The Zoom H4n also offers 4 channel mono recording, and at time of writing comes bundled with Cubase LE8.

Using a smartphone as a digital recorder

If you don't have access to a separate digital recorder, and you're not using your phone to shoot video, a simple alternative can be to use it as a digital recorder. Virtually all Apple or Android devices can be used as high quality audio recorders – either with one of the simple voice memo aps that come bundled with the IOS, or by downloading a more sophisticated app.

If set up correctly and used with a good external microphone, a smartphone can make very decent recordings. With most dedicated recording apps you'll also have the advantage of being able to send your audio files straight to your PC with blue tooth or wi-fi, rather than having to connect manually with a USB cable.

An iPhone running the TW recorder app with external mic.

Useful IOS and Android audio recorder apps.

There are a lot of free or inexpensive audio recording apps available for both of the main formats. These range from simple memo apps such as Voice Memos (Apple) or Voice Recorder (Android) through to more complex composition focused apps like Garage Band, and even apps such as Steinberg's Cubasis, which is basically a cut down, but still usable, version of the PC / MAC DAW Cubase.

Voice Memos

Cubasis

Garage Band

For basic high quality recording without too much distracting gimmickry you need something in-between. When choosing, there are a couple of features you need to look out for. A particularly important one with the kind of video sound applications we are concerned with, is the ability to provide live headphone monitoring. Many of the simpler apps don't seem to have this function, or at least it's not easy to arrange. Also, look out for recording time limits on free versions of some aps, and the types of audio file you can export. The ability to be able to adjust mic input levels is also important.

Some recorders will only record in MP3 format, which is fairly dire. You'll need something that will allow you to record WAV files with a sampling rate of at least 44100 Hz, and preferably in stereo. Apps that don't have this level of functionality can be discarded – there are plenty out there that do.

We've tried a lot of the audio apps currently on offer for both Apple IOS and Android devices, and two useful ones we've found are TwistedWave (TW) Recorder for iPhone and iPad, and Recforge lite / Recforge pro which will work on Android based smartphones and tablets.

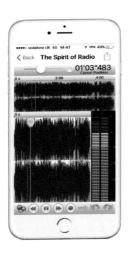

TW Recorder is a good, no-nonsense recording interface which is simple to use and gives great results. The free version of the app will record and save audio in a variety of formats, including WAV, AIFF, CAF and AAC, ALAC, FLAC and MP3. It's also possible to unlock full editing functionality, as well as more export options, such as FTP, Dropbox, Box.com and SoundCloud. However, if you're simply using the app to record and then export to your computer for editing, the free version is fine.

Recording with TW Recorder

TW Recorder is simple to use. We'll assuming you've downloaded the app to your iPhone or iPad, and you are going to record using a decent external microphone, while monitoring on headphones (see the next section on how to connect externals like this).

First, connect everything up to your device before opening the app, and if you have a powered mic, turn it on. This is because your phone or iPad is likely to default to using its internal mic, and will ignore your external one if its plugged in once the app has started up.

When you open TW Recorder you'll see a list of all the recordings you've made. This list will be blank when you first open up the app. At the bottom of this screen will be the settings button. When you use the app for the first time you'll need to tap on that and do your initial set-up.

For most of these settings the default will be fine, but it's probably best to disable iOS processing if you want to avoid Apple randomly messing with your mic settings.

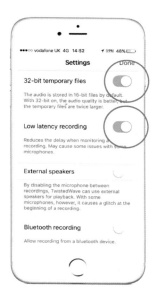

Also, unless you have a very low battery, enable **Prevent Sleeping** so that the display stays on while you are make a recording. Recording will carry on even if the display turns off, but it can be disconcerting not to have any indication that the app is still recording.

When you've set the app up, tap on the plus sign at the bottom left of the home screen. This will let you set the sampling rate of your recording.

Unless you've got a particular technical need for a high or low sample rate, just use the standard 44100 Hz and set the channel switch to stereo. You can use mono if you want to keep your file sizes down, and convert to stereo when you come to mix the audio later. A stereo file will be twice the size of a mono one.

When you tap **Done**, you'll come to the recording screen. Tap the red button to start, then quickly tap on **Pause** so that you can set your recording and headphone levels.

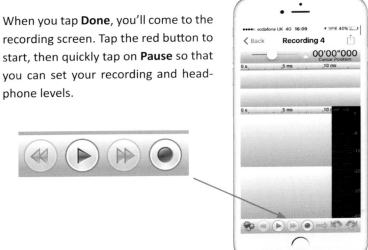

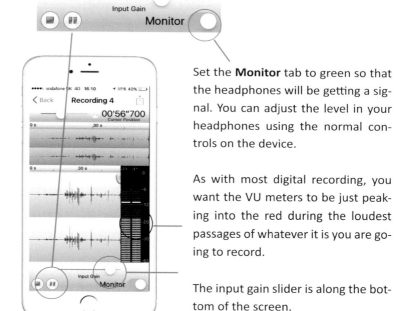

Set the **Monitor** tab to green so that the headphones will be getting a signal. You can adjust the level in your headphones using the normal controls on the device.

As with most digital recording, you want the VU meters to be just peaking into the red during the loudest passages of whatever it is you are going to record.

The input gain slider is along the bottom of the screen.

When you tap the **Record** tab again the recording will start, and an ongoing display of the audio waveform will scroll along the timeline. You can start and stop recording as many times as you like within the same file.

Unlike some recorders, you can also set the cursor to begin at any point along an already recorded timeline. Each new take then expands forwards, and the new material becomes an inserted section without recording over the audio in front of it.

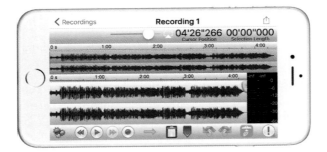

The top screen shot shows the first recording. The one below shows an expanded section and how a new inset is created without recording over the original material.

To start a completely new recording, tap **Back** at the top left of the screen and you will be taken to the home screen. Just tap on the plus sign and complete the sample rate screen as before. The file that you just recorded (here, 'recording 1') will be on the home screen list.

Exporting files.

TW Recorder includes a limited selection of editing tools. You can cut and paste sections of audio, apply some simple effects, and there's even a basic EQ.

Editing audio on a touch screen tends to be fiddly and awkward though, so the app is best used simply as a recorder. Unless you're totally stuck, just export the unedited audio files to your computer and work on them using a proper DAW or audio editor.

To export your file to your PC or Mac for editing, select it from the home screen and then tap on the export icon in the top right corner. This will take you to the export screen, which depending on whether or not you've opted for the full version of the app, will have various email and FTP options.

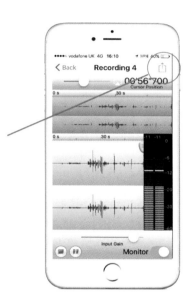

Using an external mic with a smartphone or tablet

To get the most out of recording with a smartphone or tablet, you'll need to use an external mic. Most devices apart from the newest iPhones still have a single 3.5mm audio socket that handles standard stereo headphones when used with a TRS ('tip, ring, sleeve') jack, but also allows connections for a microphone with a TRRS ('tip, ring, ring, sleeve') jack.

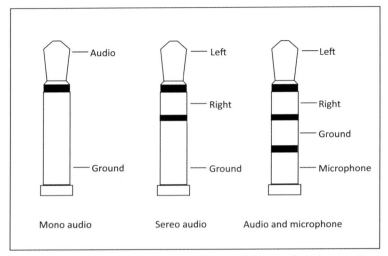

Common 3.5 mm audio jack connections

This means that connecting an external mic and headphones at the same time will usually involve some kind of adapter. Adapters that can be used with most generic devices (i.e. Android and Apple) are easy to find on the internet and will have a single TRRS jack that plugs into the smartphone or tablet, a mono TS socket to plug your mic into, and a stereo TRS socket for headphones. Adapters with XLR connectors to use with professional mics are also available, or you can easily wire one up yourself.

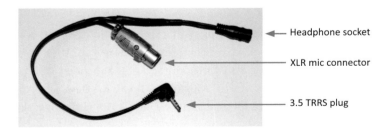

Custom made XLR and headphone adapter (see wiring diagram on next page)

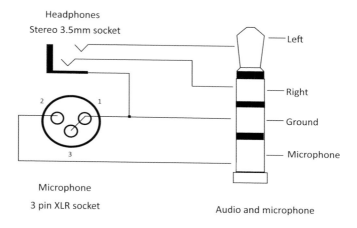

Headphones
Stereo 3.5mm socket

Left

Right

Ground

Microphone

Microphone
3 pin XLR socket

Audio and microphone

Wiring for a TRRS to XLR mic and headphone adapter

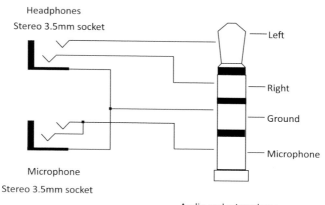

Headphones
Stereo 3.5mm socket

Left

Right

Ground

Microphone

Microphone
Stereo 3.5mm socket

Audio and microphone

Wiring for a TRRS mic and headphone adapter for 3.5mm sockets

Which mic to use?

The type of mic you use, and how you position it to get the best possible sound will really depend on what it is you are trying to record.

While there is no single type that will suit all settings, for general video work it's possible to get some quite acceptable results with a single, reasonably inexpensive directional mic such as the RODE NTG2, which can use an internal battery or phantom power if you have it available.

Common types of microphone

There are a few common types of microphone that you are likely to come across. **Dynamic** (or 'moving coil') microphones are use-

ful in a lot of situations because they tend to be quite rugged. A classic example of a **moving coil** microphone is the Sure SM58, which has been the stage vocal mic of choice for the last fifty years. This type of mic is omni-directional in that it picks up sound from all directions (see page 126), but is less sensitive to higher frequencies to either side.

Condenser mics

Condenser mic capsules are used in a whole range of studio microphones. They can be relatively fragile when compared to moving coil mics, and can't usually take high levels of sound without overloading. They make up for this with superb sound quality. Ideal for recording interviews, instruments and vocals (apart from death metal) condenser mics have a built in pre-amp and need a power supply. This is supplied by a battery in the mic body, or via a phantom power supply which needs to come from the camera or the mixer the mic is plugged into.

Electret

Because they are relatively easy to manufacture at low cost, electret mic elements are used in everything from mobile phones and multimedia headsets to telephones and digital recorders. Although they were once seen as a low-quality option, the best ones can now rival more expensive condenser mics.

An electret element of the kind that might be used as a built-in mic in a PC or phone

125

PZM

PZM mics or pressure zone microphones are basically a small electret or condenser mic element positioned near to or flush with a hard, reflective surface or 'boundary' (this type of mic is also called a boundary mic.) **PZMs** are commonly used to record full room sound by being mounted on a wall, or on large pieces of Perspex or MDF. They

can produce a natural sound with a flatter response than a free standing mic positioned at the same distance, so are great for recording live concerts or events where you want to capture the acoustics of the auditorium.

Directional features of microphones

Microphones don't all behave in the same way. Some are designed to pick up sound from all directions (**omni-directional**). Others are directional, and pick up sounds more clearly that are directly in front of them.

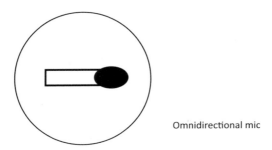

Omnidirectional mic

Bi-directional

Bi-directional mics have a figure of eight pattern which
means that they pick up sound
from in front and behind, but
reject sounds that come from
either side.

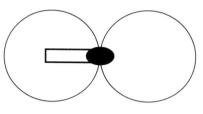

Bidirectional mic

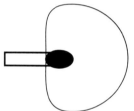

Cardioid

These mics have a have a heart shaped pattern extending towards the front.

Cardioid mic

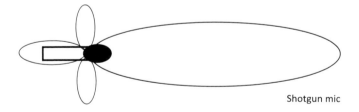

Shotgun mic

Supercardioid and hypercardioid

These mics have more extreme variations of the cardiod pattern, but
with progressively less sound rejection from the back. Shotgun mics
are used a lot in video and film work, and are highly directional.

Adding music and sound effects

You can't just use any old music you fancy in a video and upload it to the internet, although a lot of people obviously do this. If you're going to abide to the copright laws though, there are plenty of Creative Commons (CC) sites where you can get non-copyright tracks, and although a lot of the material you'll need to wade through is pretty dire, there's some really good stuff out there too if you've got the patience to find it.

A Creative Commons (CC) licence is a public copyright licence that enables the free distribution of an otherwise copyrighted work. Musicians, photographers and other artists can use a CC licence if they want to give people the right to use, and build on their work. CC gives flexibility over how material is used and as long as people abide by the conditions that are specified in the licence by which the author distributes the work they don't need to worry about copyright infringement.

CC licensed music and sounds are available through websites such as **SoundCloud** and **Freesound**, and can be used for (usually non-commercial) video and music remixing

Freesound: http://www.freesound.org
Soundcloud: https://soundcloud.com